978-0-692-88027-2

(c) 2022 Denise S'llure Publishing Company, LLC.

This Book is Dedicated to
YOU !!!

"I want to get on a Reality Show, Game Show or any show!!! But I don't know where to start!"

"I'm from a small boring town, I'll never get on television."

"I know no one famous, so I'll never get chosen for a show."

"You have to be good looking to get on Reality TV so I'm out!"

If you've ever thought like this then you NEED this book!

I will teach you how to develop what you already have in order to make you marketable for getting cast on Reality Television Shows, National Talk Shows or even becoming

a sought after Television Personality in your local market.

Before we dive deeper, I need you to understand the market that you are trying to break into. It is not called the Reality TV Market or Game Show Market. The official name is the "Non Scripted Television Market." Let me break this thing down even further. When you watch a television show such as, Power Book II: Ghost, Grey's Anatomy, etc., what you are watching are dramatized series or situation comedies,

better known as sitcoms. The commonalities of these shows are that they are in the same genre; Scripted Television.

With scripted television, the actor is essentially repeating the lines off of a script which was given to them by the producer and was written by the writing department. Scripted television can be very expensive to produce because you have to pay the Actors union scale since most of them belong to SAG (Screen Actors Guild). Then you have to have a set, pay set designers, then you have safety concerns and that's just the tip of the iceberg.

This is why many production companies are instead opting for Non Scripted Content because it is cheaper to produce. Most people who are on Reality Shows are just your ordinary person, with no Agent or Manager. They are not a part of SAG and do not come with all the expenses of a trade Actor. Therefore, the production company is saving millions on salary. Also with many forms of Non Scripted TV, there is no set or writing department. Most of the content is filmed in the participants home, or if there is a set, it is stationary and does not have all the moving compartments you will find on a television or film set.

This is important for you to know because since the Production Company saves money producing non scripted content versus scripted content, then guess what??? This means more opportunities for you to appear on TV!!! See... so all this works out in your favor.

KIMBERLY D. WORTHY

So, who am I and how do I know all of this? Let me introduce myself. I am Kimberly D. Worthy, (Television Personality, Author, Actress, Educator). Aside of all my fancy titles, I was once just a woman that took all the lemons that life threw at her and made lemonade from them. And you my reader, will be doing the same thing by the end of this book.

REMEMBER THIS

There is one point that I want you to remember more than anything else, and it is that <u>non scripted television is based on flaws</u>. No one wants to see Mr. and Mrs. Perfect on their screen. So the more flaws the better. People watch Docu-Series, Reality TV, etc. because they either connect with the personality they are watching, want to be them or watching that personality makes them feel better about their own lives. People want to be entertained and producers of the content want a cheap way to entertain them.

Think about it.....you don't watch Kim K. and her family just because they are beautiful. There are many beautiful people in the world. You watch them because they are interesting. They reveal their flaws and drama to the masses. They are uninhibited and don't care if you laugh at them or not because they know how to play the game. The more people that talk about them, positive or negative, the more money advertisers will spend to get them to promote their products. Money is the bottom line and if your flaws bring in money, then that is a positive.

Now I want you to think about your flaws. I mean really take a moment and think about them.

(Insert Dramatic Pause lol)

OK, Now write them down.

MY FLAWS

FLAW:
/flô/

By definition, a flaw is an imperfection that supposedly weakens the value of whatever it is attached to. In general this may be true, but in the world of non scripted television, your value comes from your flaws. Your flaws are what makes you YOU! That's EXCITING NEWS!!

That means that there will always be room for you on tv because it can never have enough you. You are you, and there is no one else exactly like you. I don't care if you are an identical twin. That is still not you.

I'm going to put you on game and give you an edge over every other person that wants to break in this genre. When casting directors are interviewing you for Reality Shows, Game Shows, Docu-Series, etc., they ask you open ended in depth questions about yourself. They do this to see if you can articulate what makes you unique. Most people don't even make it pass the application stage because they shy away from exposing their flaws or shortcomings. To help you better understand this, we are going to do a case study with a fictitious character named Anna.

> "But I'm tryin' to give you a million dollars worth of game for $9.99"
>
> JAY-Z

CASE STUDY

Name: Anna

Occupation: Librarian

Age: 32

Flaws/Shortcomings List
(Made by Anna)

- Shy
- Grew Up Poor
- Dyslexic
- Single Parent to a 15 year old girl

Anna's Q&A

Q1: What do you do for a living?

A: I am a Librarian.

Q2: Describe Your Personality.

A: I don't talk much. I am more on the quiet side.

Q3: Do you have any children?

A: Yes, I have a 15 year old daughter.

Q4: How was your upbringing?

A: My family didn't have much but we had love.

Q5: Have you had any challenges in your life?

A: Yes, I am dyslexic.

Ok, now let's assess this case study. Based off what you have learned thus far, do you think Anna positioned herself to standout against the thousands of other applicants who want a shot at being on television?

I want you to take a moment to really think about the answer and write it down.

If Yes....Why?

If No....Why Not?

RESULTS

Now for the correct answer. The answer is NO! If you chose no, congratulations, you're understanding the concepts14! If you chose yes, let me elaborate on what Anna could have done better to stand out.

To Anna's defense, she did tell the truth in her answers which is great, as I want you to be honest. Where Anna fell short is her lack of details in her answers. Remember, non scripted television has no official script as the title suggests. Therefore, producers are looking for people who can keep a show interesting based solely on their wit and conversation.

This means that one sentence answers are not going to cut it. When it comes to this genre, don't play it safe. Put all your cards out there and let the chips fall where they may. I want you all to re-visit Anna's flaws/shortcomings list that she made. Based off that list alone, there are at least 5 great reality shows that come to mind that she would be ideal for. So now I am going to redo Anna's Q&A list with answers that will make her stand out amongst her peers.

Types of Possible Shows for Anna

- Dating Shows for Singles

- Shows dealing with family issues

- Health Shows

- Game Shows like Jeopardy

- A mentor on a show like MTV's "Teen Mom"

Anna's Q&A

Q1: What do you do for a living?

A: I am a Librarian and earned a Masters in Library Science. I love my career and take pride in assisting students in the library. I primarily work with preteens as the library is attached to a Middle School. I've formed bonds with many of the students and some even ask my advice about school and life because they say I am easy to talk to and they trust me.

Anna's Q&A

Q2: Describe Your Personality.

A: I don't talk much. I am more on the quiet side which is very ironic being that I had to recite my dissertation in front of a board of advisors and received a standing ovation. It's also funny that all of my friends say that I am the life of the party and they tell me that what I lack with words, my facial expressions tell it all. They call me the "Shade Tree" because I throw shade silently at people.

Anna's Q&A

Q3: Do you have any children?

A: Yes. I have a 15 year old daughter whom I love very much. It was hard raising her because as you can figure by my age of only 32, I was once a teen parent. My daughter's father was never in the picture and my parents were not excited when they learned that I was expecting. Fortunately, they eventually came around and have assisted where they could with helping my daughter and I.

Q4: How was your upbringing?

A: My family didn't have much but we had love. I was the first one in my family to attend college and I am an only child. I was a very smart student and received a full scholarship to pay for college. I then worked 2 jobs to pay for Grad School along with taking out student loans.

Anna's Q&A

Q5: Have you had any challenges in your life?

A: I am dyslexic, and the irony is definitely not lost on me being a dyslexic librarian. My disability is what made me choose the career that I have. In primary school, my teachers thought I was academically behind because I had trouble reading. At that time, there wasn't much information on dyslexia. Eventually, my mom was able to get me tested from the proper individuals and that is how we learned of my condition. After that, I started to take special classes that taught me skills on how to power through my challenges and I have not looked back since.

Now do you all see the huge difference between Q&A 1 and Q&A 2? In Q&A 1, Anna shied away from discussing her flaws. She was very closed in and guarded with her answers. It was really hard to get a grasp on who she was as a person so the producers couldn't connect with her.

In Q&A 2, Anna was very open and vulnerable. She gave descriptive answers and led with her flaws. She embraced who she is as a person and was very self aware. Anna made the reader feel emotions of empathy, proudness, and humor. With answers like these, Anna strengthens her chances of being cast on a show.

Where Do I Look For Castings?

I know the burning question that you all probably have since you've learned the skills sets of being cast in non scripted content is "Where do I look for castings?" Well, there is not a straight forward answer to this question. Of course you could go to the website of the show you want to be on and look for the castings/auditions tab, but your competition is going to be fierce. That's simply because that's what most people will do. But being that you have this book at your disposal, I'm going to teach you some tricks of the trade to get the shows to come to you.

One of the best things you can do for yourself is to become an expert in something. I don't care what it is; sewing, fishing, juggling, building houses, you get the picture. You become an expert at a craft when you are not only proficient in it, but when you are able to teach the skill set to someone else. This will increase your chances of a production company casting you on a Do-it-Yourself (D.I.Y) show which are all the rave right now.

Next you're probably wondering how do you find the right production company. The answer is many times the company finds you. There are always scouts looking for people. You can use social media to help you get discovered by posting videos of yourself doing whatever you're an expert in. Research the industry you're interested in and tag your videos with those hashtags. Talent scouts follow hashtag trends.

You can also get discovered in person by making a name for yourself in your community. Remember, any press is good press. Try and get an article about yourself or business printed in your local paper. This is important because those papers usually have online editions and if your name is included in the article, now you are searchable. This puts you on the map and if you are lucky enough to snag an email address to a contact at a production company, you can use the press from the article to emphasis that you are already newsworthy.

Remember, non scripted tv relies on you keeping the viewers locked in with your winning personality. By creating your own press, it shows companies that you already have an audience interested in what you have to say and that can translate to viewers for them.

There are so many other ways to get cast on a Non Scripted TV show but that's an entirely different book. I do however provide one-on-one coaching services that teach you how to become your own publicist, which covers that more in detail.

Contact me for those services at info@kimberlydworthy.com and/or www.kimberlydworthy.com

As I mentioned earlier, before all of my fancy titles, I was once just a woman that took all the lemons that life threw at her and made lemonade.

Kimberly's Lemons into Lemonade

Growing up I was bullied, so I started using poetry to help me express my frustrations from that. This led me to writing an educational volume of poetry books called "Poetry Is Not Just Rhyming" and creating and Executive Producing the children's television show "Poetry & Life." These experiences eventually garnered me International exposure as a Keynote Speaker, Talk Show Guest, and starting an Educational business.

I am from the South and most of my family members love to cook. Unfortunately, I wasn't blessed with that skill set. I felt very inadequate and embarrassed by this but it actually worked in my favor. My lack of kitchen skills led me to starring on FOOD Network's "Worst Bakers In America" and "Worst Cooks In America."

Growing up, people would always say I had an opinion on everything and no one wanted to hear what I had to say. Well me having a strong opinion led to TMZ calling me and offering a commentator position on TMZ LIVE with Harvey Levin.

I could go on and on but you get the point. I took what some would call flaws and I led with them and the outcome has been beautiful. Now, that you have the information it is time for you to develop your YOU. This book is designed to give you general information to get you started. If ever you want to work directly with me to help you work on your YOU, I offer one-on-one sessions. Please reach out to me at info@kimberlydworthy.com and/or www.kimberlydworthy.com

Whether you work with me personally or not, it is important that you fill in this planner honestly and truthfully!

Happy Developing Your

YOU!!

DEVELOPING YOUR YOU
(PLANNER)

Q1. Why do you want to be on Non Scripted TV?

Q2. What are all the things about you that you love?

_____

_____

_____

_____

_____

_____

_____

_____

_____

_____

Q3. What are all the things about you that you hate?

Q: What are three things about you that you like?

Q4. What things about you would you change?

Q. What things would you want to change?

Q5. What are things you are embarrassed to share?

_____

_____

_____

_____

_____

_____

_____

_____

_____

_____

Q6. What do you refuse to do on television?

Q8. What do you observe during coloration?

Q7. Is there any amount of money that would make you change your mind on something you previously refused to do?

Q8. Tell me about your family.

Q9. Tell me about your past 5 relationships.

_____

_____

_____

_____

_____

_____

_____

_____

_____

_____

_____

Tell me about your past relationships.

Q10. Tell me about your friend group.

Q11. Tell me about your best friend and why they are your best friend?

Q12. Are you married? Why or Why Not?

Q8. Are you financial? Why or why not?

Q13. What is the most embarrassing thing that has happened to you?

Q25. What is meant understanding God like our best friend?

Q14. What incident in your life has made you the angriest?

_____

_____

_____

_____

_____

_____

_____

_____

_____

_____

_____

_____

Q15. How do you feel about your parents?

_____
_____
_____
_____
_____
_____
_____
_____
_____
_____
_____
_____
_____

Q: How do you feel about your parents?

Q16. What makes you unique?

Q17. If I gave you $10 Million Dollars cash today, but you had to set your best friend up for a crime that would leave them with life in prison, what would you do?

_____

_____

_____

_____

_____

_____

_____

_____

_____

_____

Q18. What do you do when you feel angry?

Q19. When and why was the last time you cried?

Q20. Since reading this book, what changes will you make in your life to help you get closer to your goal?

www.ingramcontent.com/pod-product-compliance
Lightning Source LLC
Chambersburg PA
CBHW051948160426
43198CB00013B/2355